Lingfield

in old picture postcards

by
Roger Packham

European Library – Zaltbommel/Netherlands

GB   ISBN 90 288 4795 2 / CIP

© 1989 European Library – Zaltbommel/Netherlands

INTRODUCTION

Lingfield village, tucked away in the south-east corner of Surrey close to the county boundaries with Kent and Sussex, has much to reward the observant resident and visitor. Its architectural merits have been recognised with the formation in recent years of two separate conservation areas at Plaistow Street (Gun Pond) and around the parish church.

The parish is part of Tandridge District Council, which has its offices some miles distant at Caterham and shortly to be moving to Oxted. To many residents of the Tandridge area, Lingfield is quite distant and unknown: famous for its racecourse and touched on briefly by motorists at Blindley Heath on journeys along the Eastbourne Road, but unknown.

Lingfield is today happily aware of its heritage as the creation of the conservation areas testifies and it has a long and interesting history stretching backwards beyond Domesday and the Norman Conquest. It possessed a romantic castle at Starborough with a great family dynasty of the Cobhams. Its fine church, dedicated to St. Peter and St. Paul, is indicative of a prosperous parish of some pretension. Additionally there are many fine farm houses throughout the locality which are worth seeking out for their visual delights such as timber-framing, weather boarding and mature tiles.

The coming of the railway to Lingfield just over a century ago had a considerable effect on the village and there are several roads both close to the station and further afield which were constructed within a few years of the railway's arrival. It also made possible the transportation of the racehorse for the celebrated course which dates from 1890. Other industries also benefitted and although the local railway sidings are now overgrown, evidence of the banana trade is still much in evidence in Station Road and remnants of the hop growing industry may also be seen.

Another significant product of the Victorian age was the village photographer who, apart from formal portraits of weddings and beautiful babies, also recorded scenes of village life, which from about 1900 appeared in some profusion on the ubiquitous picture postcard. This vast output of postcards has left a rich fund of pictorial evidence of how our ancestors went about their daily business.

In the era before the deification of the motor-car, these photographers, both local and national, competed with each other to produce high quality views in great quantities. In Lingfield, the local publishers included the postmaster Daniel Farrance; Arthur Martin, whose photographic shed was once visible by Gun Pond; John Jupp a local drug store and fancy repository proprietor; E.J. Skinner and the East Grinstead Photographic Company. The national publishers in competition with these gentlemen were, amongst others, Francis Frith from Reigate; W.H.Smith & Son; Valentine's and B. & S. from Enfield. There are also some outstanding cards where it is now impossible to identify their publishers.

I have arranged the book in a sequence which takes the reader from the western approach to the village, travelling along the Godstone Road towards the junction with Newchapel Road, followed by the area around Gun Pond and the High Street, before moving on the Church Town conservation area and the Victorian developments at Vicarage Road, Saxbys, Lingfield Station and the race-course. The last few photographs show some of the more important of Lingfield's outlying buildings at Moat Farm, Starborough and Haxted Mill before closing with some village groups: cricketers, pierrots and Arthur Martin's fine study of the fire brigade. I have resisted the temptation to include Dormansland, Blindley Heath, Newchapel and Horne as I hope one day to record them individually.

In compiling the brief historical notes to the photographs, I must acknowledge my debt to the Victoria County History; various issues of Kelly's Directory; Gordon Jenner's 'The Lingfield I Knew'; Peter Gray's 'Lingfield Heritage' and 'Lingfield: A Village Guide' edited by Peter Gray, Kay Percy and Chris Bale.

It is the energy of the early photographers and the golden age of the picture postcard that have made this book possible and I trust that residents and visitors alike will enjoy this record of Lingfield life from 1900 to the 1930s.

Caterham, April 1989   Roger Packham

Rustic Entrance to Lingfield.

Jupp's
Artistic Series.

1. This delightful approach to Lingfield from the west was a popular subject for postcard publishers. This card was posted in 1912 and shows the Old House and Thatched Cottage in the left foreground. They are both now listed buildings but the mature trees have disappeared. The left-hand turn is now the entrance to Wallis's garden merchants. The distant houses are numbered 50-56 Godstone Road, opposite the turn for Mount Pleasant Road.

The Thatched Cottage, Godstone Rd., Lingfield. 537

2. The two old houses from the previous page make a fine study on another postcard from 1912. The weather-boarding on the thatched cottage has now been removed to show the original fifteenth century timber framing. In 1913 Edgar Kenward was listed as a Lingfield thatcher and this view may show some of his handiwork. The Old House (left) is a fine hall house built in the late 1300s and has hardly been altered externally since 1600.

Mount Pleasant Road, Lingfield. 1345

3. This is a pre-Great War view of Mount Pleasant Road, looking north towards God-stone Road, where the houses at the end are those shown in the first photograph. The road is a late Victorian development, following the arrival of the railway to Lingfield, but the houses are more substantial than those closer to the railway station.

Lingfield, Miss Knox's Home

4. This Edwardian postcard was first published by Francis Frith in 1906 and shows The Medlars, a convalescent home run by Miss Knox, situated on the corner of Mount Pleasant Road as it sweeps around towards Newchapel Road. The card was sent to East Ham and the sender writes of having a nice change of air at this lovely place and feeling much better already.

Godstone Road, Lingfield. x94

5. Returning to the Godstone Road, this view looks eastwards towards the shops at the junction of Newchapel Road (extreme right) and was posted in 1911. The gap in the terraces before the shop blinds is now Headland Way and the first building beyond has been replaced by a modern shop.

Godstone Road, Lingfield. A861

6. This photograph was taken from outside The Lingfield Hotel a year or so before the First World War. Looking westwards, neither the photographer nor the children are in any danger from the traffic. The low wall in the middle distance fronts the William Buckwell Memorial Almshouses which were built in 1907 for six married couples and four widows. When the photo was taken, George Walter Spray was landlord of the hotel and today the single storey building on the left is a pet shop.

GODSTONE RD, LINGFIELD. 1346

7. Another Edwardian view of Godstone Road, looking west, shows some activity by the shops on a fine, sunny day. The nearest shop advertises Colman's Starch and today it has a modern shop-front for a turf accountancy. The semi-detached house in the centre has lost its sash-windows now and the white house on the right has become an estate agents with one central doorway. It won an environmental award in 1980 but the tree and the neat wall have been swept away.

Newchapel Road, Lingfield.

Jupp's
Artistic Series. 942.

8. John Jupp's charming postcard shows nine Lingfield children in the foreground of this view, which was posted in 1916. The old house on the left has vanished and the neat hedges have disappeared. They have been replaced by some dreary flats and a petrol station. The building in the distance is now The Old Cage public house and although Lincolns Mead, a modern cul-de-sac, has been built on the right, Bricklands Farm and Ormuz Cottages (1894) lend some character to this part of Newchapel Road.

Lingfield.

9. This Frith postcard of 1905 was taken from the Godstone Road looking towards Plaistow Street with Newchapel Road on the right. A child stands outside Mr. and Mrs. Halsey's butcher's and greengrocery shops whilst a horse-drawn furniture pantechnicon stands outside the Greyhound Inn whose landlord at this time was Benjamin Boorer. A featureless modern semi-detached house now stands on the site of the house on the left. Compare the above shops with the replacement building shown in the next photograph.

LINGFIELD. PLAISTOW STREET.

10. This 1920s view shows the replacement shops at the junction of Newchapel Road and Plaistow Street (see previous photograph). It was published by E.M. Green, The Library, Lingfield, whose shop is shown above on the left. The gargoyles at the apex of each gable are an interesting feature but the building lacks the charm of its predecessor which was featured in John Hassell's painting of 1822.

"Pans Pocket" The crafts corner of a 16th. Century House, Lingfield.

11. This is another 1920s postcard and shows the buildings which now form the Old Cage public house, opposite the Greyhound. At this time the buildings were a crafts shop and a café, the former proving a great attraction for children. Before the Great War it had been Milton Batchelar's grocery and general shop. Mr. Batchelar also collected the poor rate for several years and would no doubt be surprised to know that these two buildings have been converted to form an inn.

12. A horse-drawn vehicle, preceded by a cyclist, makes its way past the Greyhound in a Frances Frith postcard of 1903. The shop on the left is Playstowe Hall, built in 1885, and its sign advertises Lingfield Drug Stores. The stores were run by John Jupp who also advertised a fancy repository and today it houses a furnishing shop and fuel merchants. In the centre is today's Cage public house, dating from 1592, and the building on the right is Rose Cottages on the corner of Vicarage Road. These cottages show a pleasing contrast of weather boarding and tile hanging.

Plaistow Street,
JUPP, PHOTO, LINGFIELD.
Lingfield, Surrey.

13. This Jupp postcard, which dates from about 1905, shows the Lingfield Drug Stores (Playstowe Hall) from the opposite direction to that in the previous photograph. It is looking eastwards and the photographer was standing in the garden of Rose Cottages. The row of white cottages on the right have all been demolished. The old lock-up cage and the forge (centre) may be seen in the distance.

Old Cage, Lingfield.

Jupp's Photo Series

14. This is an unusual close-up of the old cage in Jupp's photo series of about 1912. A workman sits inside with a collection of road signs whilst a prop encourages the ancient oak tree away from the roof of the cage. This little building dates back to 1773 and was used for many years as a lock-up for local wrong doers. Its last detainees were some poachers in 1882.

15. Two gentlemen pause for a conversation, untroubled by any form of traffic, on a summer's day probably in the 1920s. Looking westwards, the buildings shown are all much loved features of Lingfield in their different styles. They are, from the left, the Old Cage, Rose Cottages and St. Peter's Cross with the little single storey shop behind. The cross is believed to date from the fifteenth century and marks the centre of the Plaistow Street Conservation Area.

16. The East Grinstead Photo Company produced this fine view in about 1913. It shows the turning for Vicarage Road by the neat hedge of Rose Cottages and the narrow roadway on the north side of Gun Pond. The little shop advertises hair cutting and R. White's lemonade and the eye is drawn skywards towards two monkey puzzle trees and a row of tall telegraph poles. Behind the shop is Billshurst Cottages and in front of the fence guarding the pond can be seen some water pipes awaiting burial.

478 THE CAGE, ST PETER'S CROSS, LINGFIELD

17. Two youths in caps give a passing glance to a gentleman reading a newspaper, possibly at the photographer's request. This 1920s view shows the hedge of Rose Cottages curving into Vicarage Road with Billshurst Cottages to the right of St. Peter's Cross. The house on the right is Hope Cottage and its sign board advertises 'J. Hood: House Decorator'. In an earlier directory John Hood is described as a plumber.

VILLAGE POND AND CAGE, LINGFIELD.

18. This postcard was sent to Fred Picknell at Chatham by his father who was enjoying a day at Lingfield races on 7th April 1916. Hope Cottage is framed by two mature oak trees whilst on the right the shed-like photographic premises belonging to Arthur Martin may be seen. Mr. Martin recorded much of Lingfield life in the early years of this century.

19. A horse may be seen on the right, staring into the Pond, with the village forge behind him in this postcard by Jupp posted in 1904 from the Colony, Lingfield. The blacksmith at this time was William Terry. The weather-boarded building on the left was for many years Farrance's grocers, drapers and wine merchants. Daniel Farrance was also the village postmaster.

THE CAGE AND THE MEMORIAL. LINGFIELD.

20. This card was posted in 1935 and shows an Eldorado Ice Cream salesman in the centre of the picture. To the right of the tall war memorial is a box belonging to the Lingfield District First Aid Society. The cottages on the opposite side of the road are preceded by a large advertising poster which a passing cyclist safely ignores. The cottages on the left would have made a valuable addition to the conservation area.

The Village Pond and War Memorial, Lingfield.

1133.

B. & S.
ENFIELD.

21. Three Lingfield ladies stand in front of Gun Pond and Arthur Martin's studio in a post-card dated 1931. Hope Cottage stands to the right of the war memorial. The trees and long coats indicate a winter's day and the scene is remarkable for the absence of traffic and street furniture.

WAR MEMORIAL, LINGFIELD.

22. Following the destruction of the Great War, this postcard features the Lingfield War Memorial. It is of Portland stone and was erected in 1920 at a cost of about £500. It consists of a base surmounted by an octagonal pillar bearing a lantern with a perpetual light.

23. This postcard was published by D.W. Farrance, grocer and general furnisher, Lingfield, in about 1905. Looking south-west, it is interesting to see the series of advertisements in front of the cottages beyond Gun Pond. Note the props around the cage which support the old oak tree.

PLAISTOW ST. LINGFIELD. 1340

24. The hedges and uneven fences of the Plaistow Street cottages are clearly shown in this view towards East Grinstead Road on a postcard dated 1915. The cottages have sadly been replaced by the modern development known as The Row. The buildings in the centre of the photograph are on the corner of East Grinstead Road and have also been replaced. The only building which survives today can be seen to the left of the picture and is now known as Lion House.

Plaistow Street, Lingfield.

Pub. by E. J. Skinner, Lingfield.

25. The tile hung house in the centre is Magnus Deo as it appeared in about 1905. The house dates from the seventeenth century and possesses a large inglenook fireplace. Beyond Magnus Deo can be seen buildings which were once Stanford's Corn Stores, now replaced by the modern parade of shops in East Grinstead Road. Note the milk churn vehicle at the extreme left.

High Street, Lingfield.

Jupp's Photo Series.

26. An advertisement for Mazawattee Tea holds a prominent place on the wall of Farrance's Stores on this Jupp postcard which was posted in 1911. Both oak trees and the wooden railings have disappeared but the post office building on the right is easily recognisable. The building on the left is today's J. & K. Fine Foods and its window has been altered but retains the same outline. Beyond Farrance's Stores, the left-hand side of the High Street has little in common with the same view of today.

HIGH STREET. LINGFIELD.

27. This postcard dates from about 1930 and shows the increase in traffic and traffic signs compared to many of the earlier views. The grocer's delivery van from East Grinstead is standing outside Castle's Stores (late Farrance's) and the postcard provides a glimpse of the north side of the High Street before re-development. The monkey puzzle tree competes with the telegraph pole to be the tallest object in the photograph.

28. Two boys waiting outside Lingfield post office on a summer's day are photographed for a postcard dated September, 1914. The post office is much the same today but the shop on the left-hand side is now occupied by a ladies' hairdresser.

High Street, Lingfield. ×06

29. This postcard is a companion to the previous view and was posted in August, 1913. It shows the shops on the south side of the High Street which, unlike the buildings opposite, are still instantly recognisable. The youth in the picture is probably a telegram boy and the advertisement beyond the post office building reads: 'Lingfield Bakery: A.G. Finch, Pastry Cook and Confectioner; Cakes and Pastry of Every Description; Refreshments.' The premises are still occupied by a baker.

Lingfield.

30. Progressing further eastwards along the High Street, this view by Francis Frith & Co., which was taken in 1903, captures the unfamiliar buildings on the north side of the street leading towards the schools. The shop on the immediate right was Albert Boorer's butcher's shop and beyond can be seen Walter Maxwell's hairdresser's and W.M. Leach, an auctioneer and estate agent. A sign outside the hairdresser's advertises the re-covering and repointing of umbrellas.

31. Another postcard by Frith shows Lingfield High Street, looking westwards on a card posted to Antwerp in 1907. Boorer's and Finch's shops appear on the left-hand side (Leeds Terrace, built in 1893) but the site of the post office is graced by a handsome Lingfield oak. Opposite, Farrance's cart is parked in front of Farrance's Stores which displays advertisements for Colman's Mustard and Colman's Starch. Magnus Deo may be seen beyond the white railings at centre.

32. This postcard was published by D.W. Farrance and although posted in 1916, it was no doubt produced several years earlier. There are thirteen people in the photograph and they are all looking at the photographer who is standing, quite safely, in the middle of the road by the turning for Talbot Road on the left. Note the tall telegraph poles and the monkey puzzle tree.

33. This 1920s view, by E.M. Green, The Library, Lingfield, shows a single vehicle parked outside the Lingfield Garage, which at this time was owned by H.P. Clayton. Farrance's Stores has been taken over by Edward Castle to become Castle's Stores. The distant house (centre) is Magnus Deo and to its right can be seen the building which today is The Wine Stores.

High Street, Lingfield.

34. This lively postcard by B. & S., Enfield, shows a familiar view of the High Street in about 1914. The shop fronts have altered, inevitably and the International Stores has given way to a video shop. The fish shop and L.J. Hambleton's have become a french restaurant and a hair stylist and beyond Talbot Road, Rupert Chandler's outfitters (Paris House) is now occupied by John Banks.

The Schools, Lingfield.   635.

35. In 1915, this postcard was sent to Percy Godley at a Military Hospital in Dover, no doubt a casualty of the Great War. The above buildings are now Lingfield Middle School but for many years this was Lingfield Mixed and it was built in 1860, extended in 1906. In 1913, William Abell was the master and it is likely that the house on the right was his residence.

The Schools, Lingfield.

36. E.J. Skinner of Lingfield published this view of The Schools on a postcard dated 1906 which shows the buildings before the enlargements which were made in 1906-7. The Lingfield Infants School, on the right, was built in 1849 and at the time of the enlargements, the mistress was Ellen Quigley who was succeeded by Elizabeth Woodley in about 1912.

37. Lingfield Council School-Infants is shown here on an postcard dated 1913. Its appearance has altered somewhat from the previous photograph and the turret has disappeared. The card was sent to Miss Wright at The School House, Ash, near Wrotham from Lena of 12, Clinton Terrace, Dormansland. The Infants School is now used as The Lingfield Centre.

1183.   Church Walk, Lingfield.

B. & S.
ENFIELD

38. B. & S. Enfield published this postcard of Church Walk in the 1920s. The walk is much the same today and starts from the High Street by the schools and leads to the conservation area around the church. An earlier postcard of the same locality by Jupp refers to the walk as Ashpit Lane.

Victoria Memorial Institute, Lingfield, Surrey.

JUDP PHOTO. LINGFIELD

39. This building, now known as The Lingfield Victoria Club, is in the High Street, opposite The Lingfield Centre, and is here captured on a postcard dated 1905. The Victoria Memorial Institute was erected in 1901 by public subscription and the stone at the front was laid by Sydney Austin, M.R.C.S. who was medical officer and vaccinator for the Lingfield District. The institute, which cost about £1,500, was built by Ernest Stanford, a local builder, and contained reading rooms and a library of over 500 volumes. It was enlarged in 1906 at a further cost of £500.

40. Leaving the High Street, our journey takes us down Church Road to the second of Lingfield's Conservation Areas. The buildings grouped around the Parish Church of St. Peter and St. Paul are captured here in a Frith postcard of about 1904. The building on the right is the old Star public house which has since moved across the road to a new building. The landlord at this time was Walter Wigmore. Three little girls stand in the road with their hoops which were very popular with Edwardian children.

41. Arthur Martin has photographed The Star on this postcard which bears a postmark of 1904. The letter box on the wall remains there to this day but the little building with the tall chimney in front of Pollard House (left) has been demolished. The two little boys are aware of the photographer but the two men appear to be more concerned with their cigarettes.

42. Mr. Martin's photograph shows The Star at the turn of the century before the extension was added towards the white fencing. Between Pollard House (extreme left) and the church can be seen another unfamiliar building, destined to be burnt down. Most of the girls queueing behind the donkey cart are looking directly at the photographer.

S 5278   CORNER OF OLD VILLAGE, LINGFIELD.

43. A Kingsway postcard by W.H. Smith, published in about 1910, shows the old-fashioned way that butcher's used to display their produce — no doubt unhygienic for present day tastes. Beyond Mr. Faulkner's shop may be seen Pollard Cottage and then Old Town House, the latter being the replacement building for that shown in the previous view. The butcher's is now a private residence.

Old Church Entrance.   Lingfield Surrey

44. This attractive card by Jupp was posted in 1907 and shows Old Town House, on the left, as it appeared before the disastrous fire early this century. Originally a late sixteenth century timber-framed house, it underwent a re-building in about 1908. Note the untiled appearance of the end gable in comparison to photograph number 43.

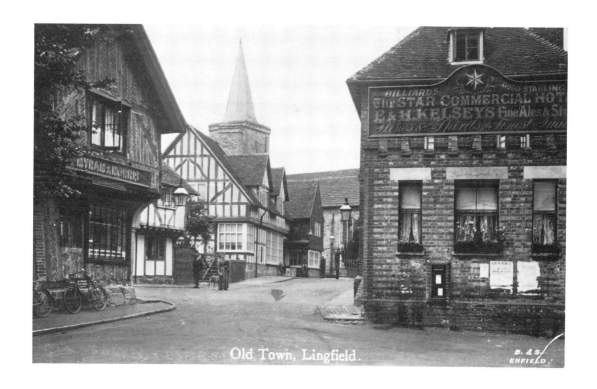

Old Town, Lingfield.

B. & S.
ENFIELD

45. Messrs. Myram and Morris have taken over Faulkner's butcher's shop in Pollard House and two delivery bicycles may be seen outside. A man stands in front of an advertisement for Barclay's Stout and Ales (left) whilst The Star boasts E. & H. Kelsey's Fine Ales which were brewed in Tunbridge Wells. The card was posted in 1926 but would appear to date from about 1912.

In the Old Town, Lingfield.

46. This postcard was produced in J. Jupp's Sepia Series and was posted in 1920. The photographer has his back to the church and is looking towards Myram and Morris's butchers, observed as always, by the local children. The attractive row of cottages on the left-hand side are Church Gate Cottage and Star Cottages.

Churchyard Entrance, Lingfield.

Jupp's Photo Series, 160

47. John Jupp's postcard, dated 1915, shows the churchyard looking away from the church porch towards Church Gate Cottage on the left and Old Town Cottage, right. It is interesting to note that the gravestone to the left of the picture marks the resting place of James Thomas (1802-1886), the Vicar of the Parish for seventeen years.

Lingfield Church.

48. Frith's postcard, sent to Lamberhurst in 1907, shows an unusual view of St. Peter and St. Paul's from the north-west. The stables to the right have been demolished and the pond in the foreground is no more. The building on the left is The College, now situated in College Close.

NORTH ENTRANCE,

LINGFIELD CHURCH.

49. The entrance to the parish church is shown here from Vicarage Road, with Barn Cottage on the left and the Guest House (right) in about 1912. At the time of the photograph, the latter was described as the Old Guest Hall and was lived in by Mrs. Hayward. It is now the public library and the building dates from the late 1400s, heavily restored in 1900.

S 5286   OLDE GUEST HALL, LINGFIELD

50. This Kingsway postcard by W.H. Smith was posted from Lingfield in 1910 and shows two local girls in front of the Old Guest Hall before its present use as a public library. The house is reputedly the guest house of Lingfield College and is a good example of a Wealden house.

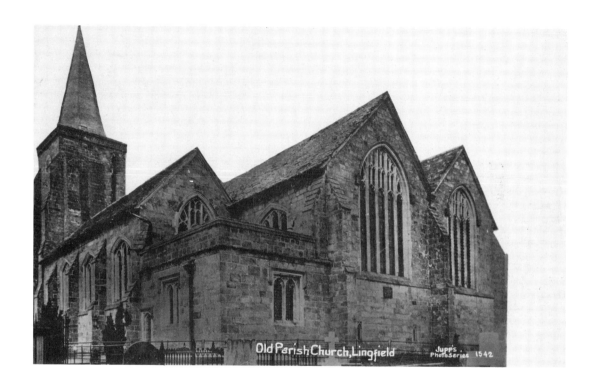

Old Parish Church, Lingfield
Jupp's Photo Series 1542

51. Jupp's postcard of the old parish church was posted in 1919 but was no doubt published before the Great War. The church, dedicated to St.Peter and St. Paul, is in the perpendicular style which is unusual in Surrey. The oldest part of the church is the tower and part of the west wall, which are both fourteenth century. The main re-building of the church took place in 1431.

Tomb of
First Lord Cobham
& Old Lectern,
Lingfield Church.

Jupp's
PhotoSeries. 941.

52. Inside Lingfield Church are many interesting tombs and brasses and in this Jupp post-card of about 1912, the tomb of the first Lord Cobham is depicted. He was responsible for the fortification of the original Starborough Castle in 1342. The chained bible (right) was given to the parish by W. Saxby in 1688.

"Old Barn Studio and Pleasaunce;" Lingfield Surrey.

JUPP, PHOTO, LINGFIELD.

53. Jupp's postcard, which was posted in 1907, shows seven Edwardian boys at the top of the steps with the Guest House on the left. The building in the centre of the photograph is now known as Barn Cottage. Note the old fashioned headboard style of grave on the extreme right.

Surrey.

Lingfield Vicarage,

JUPP PHOTO LINGFIELD

54. This attractive Victorian building is Lingfield Vicarage as it appeared on a Jupp post-card, postally used in 1906. At this time the vicar was Reverend Kenneth Clarke M.A. who held the living from 1904 until 1911 when he was succeeded by Reverend Alfred Pitt Gutch. A modern building now serves as Lingfield Vicarage.

Lower Vicarage Rd. Lingfield. 1354

55. This view shows what is now Vicarage Road and was published in about 1910. The houses nearest to the camera are numbers 23 and 24 and although the gate and style no longer remain, a footpath continues to serve as the way to Woodlands.

56. A horse and cart wait outside Sitford & Son's grocers on an sunny day in about 1913. Bakers Lane leads away to the right and Saxbys Lane curves away to the left. Sitford's has become a solicitor's and the tree has been removed. The first three houses in Saxbys Lane are Eastbourne House, Cavendish House and Pier Cottages and they were all built in 1884.

57. Proceeding along Saxbys Lane towards Crowhurst Road, the photographer is following the progress of the horse and cart shown in the previous photograph. The photographer was standing by the modern Haywardens and the house on the left is Cypress Cottage. The weather boarded building in the centre has been replaced by maisonettes (numbers 49-79) and a new fire station.

58. The local boys obligingly pose for the photographer in Station Road in about 1910. The house on the left is number 11 and the little shop is still trading from the same position today. It was built as Alma Cottage in 1888, shortly after the railway arrived at Lingfield.

Lingfield Railway Station.

59. F. Frith & Co produced this view of Lingfield Railway Station and its staff in 1906. The London, Brighton and South Coast Railway Company built the line from Croydon to East Grinstead in 1884 and the station at Lingfield had considerable influence on the development of the locality. At the time of the photograph, George Crittenden was station master.

Railway Station.

Pub. by E. J. Skinner, Lingfiel

60. This view of Lingfield Station was published by E.J. Skinner and this postcard was posted in 1905. The signal gantry has disappeared and the iron footbridge has been removed to the Bluebell Railway. Some smiling youths can just be seen behind the gate to the left.

THE STATION. LINGFIELD.

61. This view of the station, looking north, is by an unidentified publisher and includes some interesting features which are no longer visible. These include the canopies on the central island platform, the sidings to the right of the picture and the gas lamp posts. Note the signal box beneath the footbridge.

NEW PLACE, LINGFIELD. 1516

62. Opposite Lingfield Station stands the impressive New Place and it is featured here in a postcard dated 1912. Unusually built of stone, the entrance porch bears the date 1617. At the time of the photograph New Place was lived in by Miss Hall F.L.S., F.Z.S.

Town Hill, Lingfield.

63. Looking eastwards towards the racecourse, Town Hill is shown here at its junction with Church Road and Camden Road (right) on a summer's day in the 1920s. The house just visible is Fair Oaks (now a dentist) and a similar scene today would doubtless include local traffic travelling to and from Dormansland.

Entrance to Racecourse, Lingfield.

1129.

B. & S.
ENFIELD.

64. This is another 1920s view by B. & S. Enfield showing the entrance to the famous racecourse following the descent along Town Hill as shown in the previous photograph. It is a summer's day and there is still no threat to the pedestrians from motor vehicles.

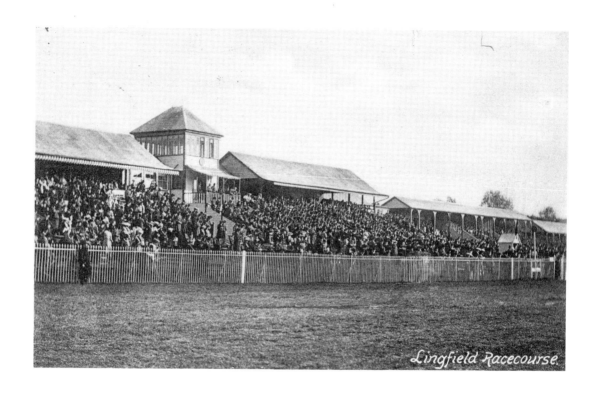

Lingfield Racecourse.

65. Francis Frith published this postcard of Lingfield Racecourse in 1903 which shows the well-populated grandstands. The racecourse was established in 1890 and a straight mile course was laid out three years later. The Clerk of the Course in Edwardian times was Robert Fowler.

Lingfield Racecourse.

66. Another Frith postcard shows a typical scene on race day in 1903. The course boasted telegraph offices, several luncheon rooms, kitchens and stabling for over one hundred horses with dormitories for stable lads. The Earl of Durham and the Earl of Dudley were members of the committee of the Lingfield Park Club at this time.

The Racecourse,   Lingfield Park, Surrey.

JUPP, PHOTO LINGFIELD,

67. John Jupp's locally published postcard shows a race in progress and was posted to Ireland in 1909. At this time there were enclosures for carriages and motors and one for the Royal Automobile Club. In addition there were members and 'Tattersall's' stands and other stands for the public, press and trainers.

STANHOPE COTTAGES, LINGFIELD. 1520

68. Stanhope Cottages are photographed in about 1910. The road leads back towards the racecourse which lies on the far side of the railway bridge. The cottages remain much the same today although there are some new roof tiles in evidence to replace the original slate.

IVY HOUSE, LINGFIELD. 1952

69. This Edwardian view of Ivy House will appeal to pupils and former pupils of Notre Dame Senior School for it now forms part of the Sixth Form Centre of Lingfield's best known educational establishment, in St. Piers Lane. At the time of the publication of the postcard, Ivy House was the private residence of Philip Edward De Clermont.

Old St Pier's Farm   The Colony Lingfield Surrey

JUPP PHOTO LINGFIELD.

70. St. Piers Farm, now part of the Hospital School, is shown here on a postcard by Jupp as it appeared in the early part of the century. It was then known as The Colony and was the home for epileptic children. The old farm house dates from about the year 1500 and was originally a four bay hall house.

The Moat, Lingfield. 527

71. This handsome Georgian house which is now known as Moat Farm is shown here on a postcard dating from about 1912. It is visible across the fields to the north of Godstone Road and the boundaries of three parishes meet within the house. The moat has been largely filled in but the pond makes for a fine setting.

Starborough Castle.   Lingfield, Surrey.

72. Starborough Castle appears on this Jupp postcard of about 1905. An impressive castle was built in the fourteenth century and demolished by Oliver Cromwell in about 1650, although the moat is still visible. The above house is strictly Starborough House rather than Castle and dates from the middle of the eighteenth century. Louis XII of France was a captive in the original castle after the battle of Agincourt.

73. The East Grinstead Photo Company produced this postcard of Haxted Mill which was posted in 1912. The weather-boarding makes the mill particularly attractive and it now serves as a museum of milling history and has its own restaurant. Haxted Mill House, beyond the mill, is much older than its Victorian appearance indicates. The building to the left of the picture has been demolished.

Martin, Photo. Edenbridge and Lingfield.

THE LINGFIELD PIERROT TROUPE.

74. Arthur Martin has produced a postcard of the local pierrots as they appeared in Edwardian times. Pierrots were French pantomime characters and itinerant minstrels with whitened faces and loose, white costumes and they enjoyed much popularity at this time.

75. Lingfield boys proudly display a Challenge Shield for their cricket prowess on another fine study by Arthur Martin. Cricket has a long history in this part of Surrey and a record exists of Lingfield beating London in 1739. Note the uniform shirts of the youthful Lingfield eleven.

76. It is appropriate that Arthur Martin's photograph of the Lingfield Fire Brigade, resplendent in their brass helmets, brings this selection of Lingfield photographs to a conclusion. The original fire station was housed opposite the old Star public house and a photograph of it exists in Gordon Jenner's 'The Lingfield I knew' (1980).